Original title:
Apple Core Secrets

Copyright © 2025 Creative Arts Management OÜ
All rights reserved.

Author: Evan Hawthorne
ISBN HARDBACK: 978-1-80586-412-7
ISBN PAPERBACK: 978-1-80586-884-2

Layers of Time

Peeling back the years, what do we find?
A tale of laughter, colors entwined.
Each bite reveals a story to share,
A crunchy delight, floating in air.

Fragrant memories of days gone by,
A little bit serious, but oh so spry.
Digesting the past with a witty grin,
Savoring life with each juicy spin.

Beneath the Rind

Beneath the rind, secrets do play,
Jokes and giggles hidden away.
You'd never know, just take a bite,
A punchline waits, oh what a sight!

A fruity laugh that's hard to crack,
Puns all around, and none look back.
Chomp down hard and what do you get?
A fruit-filled laugh that you'll never forget!

Aroma of History

The scent of laughter, sweet and bright,
Dancing on tongues in the soft daylight.
Fragrant whispers from trees long gone,
Making us chuckle with every dawn.

In the garden of jest, the past does bloom,
A banquet of giggles is filling the room.
Taste the folly, the jokes on display,
Aromatic riddles that brighten the day!

The Uncut Secrets

In the heart of the fruit, frolic some jest,
Uncut secrets that tickle the chest.
One slice reveals what's clever and sly,
The fruit of laughter makes spirits fly.

Lurking within each innocent core,
Are jests that had everyone begging for more.
With giggles and grins, we feast on delight,
Where humor erupts in the mid-summer night!

Lifting the Veil of Skin

In the kitchen, a fruit parade,
A shiny red orb, in sunlight played.
With a twist and a turn, my lips will meet,
Crunching the sweetness, oh what a treat!

But look closer now, what's that I see?
A secret inside, just waiting for me.
Not just a snack, but tales to tell,
Of seeds and whispers, in fruity gel.

The peeling reveals more than just taste,
A comedy show, let's not waste!
With every bite, it giggles and squawks,
I've unearthed the fruit that actually talks!

Now friends gather round, with jaws dropped wide,
As I share the laughs that this fruit cannot hide.
Lifting the veil, what wonders abound,
In a simple red fruit, giggles are found!

In the Shadow of Trees

Beneath the branches wide and green,
A fruit was lost, if you know what I mean.
It rolled away with a cheeky grin,
Oh, what a mess, let the laughs begin!

Squirrels looked on with curious eyes,
As I searched the ground for its thin disguise.
The fruit was sneaky, playing the fool,
But oh, the giggles were wonderfully cool!

Crisp Confessions

In the kitchen, a crime did unfold,
The fruit on the table was loud and bold.
With each crisp bite, I let out a squeal,
What a slippery secret—let's make a deal!

The seeds were plotting a silly escape,
Right there in my snack, they began to reshape.
With a wink and a nod, they laughed in delight,
Who knew that munching could end with a fight?

Kernels of Wisdom

Tiny seeds hidden under the skin,
Sharing their tales while I munch and grin.
They whispered secrets of juicy delight,
But puns on their names? Oh, what a sight!

With each little bite came a shifty chuckle,
The fruit made me giggle with every small struggle.
Wisdom is funny when you take a knell,
In this fruity saga, all's well that ends well!

Beyond the Crunch

There's laughter hidden in every crunch,
With bites that ring like a silly punch.
When chomping down, do you hear the cheer?
It's a zany party, let's all gather near!

As juice drips down, we share tales so wild,
Each slice telling stories, both silly and guiled.
In this cheerful feast, let's never feel shy,
For laughter is sweet, and oh my, oh my!

Forbidden Delights

In the kitchen, a shiny red,
A treat so sweet, but should be fed.
Whispers of flavor, they know too well,
But oh, the tales they never tell.

Peeking through leaves, a snack divine,
Chomp and giggle, like it's a crime.
Savory bites with a hint of glee,
Who knew munching could be so free?

Nectar of Truth

Beneath the skin, a juicy lie,
Sips of sweetness that make you sigh.
Giggles echo from each crisp bite,
Truths in the juice, oh what a sight!

The juiciest gossip, it all spills out,
With every chew, laughter's about.
Bite-sized wonders, secrets galore,
Fruity confessions we can't ignore.

Rustling Memories

In the orchard, children play,
Beneath the branches where shadows sway.
Crunching laughter with every fall,
Kernels of joy, we savor them all.

Tickling leaves, a breezy cheer,
Every nibble holds friendship near.
Whispers of times when we were wild,
Memories fresh, just like a child.

The Hidden Kernel

In the heart of the fruit, a secret lies,
Nestled deep, beneath the size.
Biting through layers, oh what a find,
Wit and whimsy all intertwined.

Crunching kernels, a playful jest,
Giggles bloom, we're truly blessed.
From tart to sweet, twists of fate,
It's fun to share, never too late!

Tales from the Orchard Floor

Beneath the tree, a treasure found,
A quirky pit, in grass it's bound.
What's left behind, a taste of jest,
Insects laugh, they know it best.

Who dropped this gem? A creature small,
With tiny hands, or none at all?
The worms in jest, they do rejoice,
In this odd world, we've made our choice.

With every bite, a giggle sprouts,
Juices fly, and laughter shouts.
A squishy prize, so much delight,
An orchard's tale, a funny sight.

A Slice of Enigma

What hides within the juicy shell?
Mysteries that none can tell.
Each crisp bite a riddle spun,
A game of flavors, who has won?

The peanut butter's jealous stare,
As jelly slinks, it's unaware.
Squirrels chatter, dreams of pie,
While my moonbeams dance and fly.

Honey drips from secret jars,
While laughter twinkles like the stars.
Every crumb a tale unfolds,
In slices stacked, the truth beholds.

Unearthed Within

Beneath the branches, secrets lie,
Old stories whispered from nearby.
The cider's punch, a playful fight,
With giggles shared under moonlight.

What's buried here? A joke or two,
A nut that thought it had a clue.
With roots that wiggle, and stems that twist,
It hopes to shine, it hopes to gist.

A garden of whimsy, fresh and weird,
Beneath the soil, the laughter steered.
In every bite, surprises go,
A funny dance from 'neath the glow.

Forbidden Flavors

A taste of mischief on my tongue,
Crunchy tales that must be spun.
The label says, "Do not explore,"
But who can resist? It's hard to bore!

The golden hue, a grin so wide,
Peeking through leaves, it tries to hide.
While critters plot their daring heist,
Delight in flavors that entice!

With every splash, a giggle blooms,
In secret nooks or leafy rooms.
Laughter bubbles, sweet and bold,
In every snack, a tale retold.

Forgotten Bites

Once I had a snack so ripe,
In my haste, I took a type.
I bit down deep, it was a mess,
Left with crumbs and much distress.

Thought I lost a tasty prize,
Checked my pockets, what a surprise!
Half a slice, a slimy lump,
My lunch had turned into a dump.

The Essence Within

Peeling layers with delight,
What's inside? A sweet respite!
Wonders dwell in every bite,
A twist of fate, oh what a sight!

Juicy tales that make me grin,
Magic bursts from deep within.
What's the point, just take a look,
Life's a joke, a funny book!

Nature's Hidden Truths

Underneath that shiny skin,
Lies the truth where laughs begin.
Every crunch a giggle grows,
In the bite, a secret flows.

Nature laughs with every chew,
Dancing whispers, just for you.
Peep inside, don't be shy,
Find the chuckles hidden nigh.

The Core of Mystery

In the center, what's the score?
A riddle wrapped in fruity lore.
Giggling seeds with tales to tell,
Inside this fruit, there's magic spell.

Can you guess what's hiding there?
Maybe crumbs or a funny bear?
Life's a joke, enjoy the ride,
As laughter waits where taste resides.

Depths of the Orchard

Beneath the boughs, they whisper low,
The tales of fruit that nobody knows.
A worm in a hat, discussing his plan,
To steal shiny apples, yes, oh man!

Bouncing and tumbling, the critters convene,
In hushed tones they plot over apples unseen.
A squirrel with dreams of a pie oh so grand,
Jostles a rabbit, makes fruitcake in sand.

Secrets in the Garden

In the garden, the gnomes take a peek,
Sneaky and sly, they don't dare to speak.
Behind every bush, they dig out a scheme,
To brew fizzy cider from a grasshopper's dream.

The ladybugs laugh with a wink and a grin,
As visions of orchard games all begin.
While bees buzz around with a comical guise,
Stirring sweet nectar filled with surprise.

Beyond the Rind

With gutsy giggles, the peelers unite,
They dance through the groves, what a curious sight!
Exchanging the tales of a bruised fruit delight,
As laughter erupts in the warm autumn night.

One whispered rumor, it's chaos at hand,
That pears hold a meeting to start a rock band!
With melodies sweet, they'll strum on their tarts,
Captivating the critters and stealing their hearts.

Mysteries in the Flesh

What lurks inside, when the fruit's sliced anew?
Baffling secrets no one ever knew.
Like a scary movie with seeds in the plot,
Or a picnic gone wrong, all tangled in rot.

The fruits hold a riddle, as juicy as jest,
With puns so ripe, they'll surely impress.
A bite and a chuckle, as flavors collide,
The mysteries bloom, laughter swells inside.

Seeds of Knowledge

In my garden, I plant a dream,
Little seeds with a quirky gleam.
They wiggle and giggle in the dirt,
Waiting for sun, but first, a spurt!

One says, 'I'm a wisdom sprout!'
Another claims, 'I'll rule, no doubt!'
They plot and scheme in the soil's bed,
Confusing roots with thoughts in their head.

Rain comes down, they start to rise,
With silly hats and gleeful sighs.
Knowledge blooms in colors bright,
A banquet for worms, quite the sight!

So here's to seeds of all delight,
Sprouting dreams in day and night.
With laughter, they lighten the weight,
For wisdom's fun, just take the bait!

The Heart of the Harvest

In the orchard, we dance around,
A fruity festival, joy abound!
With baskets full and cheeks so round,
Stumbling o'er laughter on the ground.

A pear's a tease and a plum's a prank,
While cherries wink on the fruity tank.
Beneath the trees, we share our jokes,
As nutty squirrels steal our yolks!

The harvest king, with crown of vines,
Toasts the fruit with silly lines.
He jests about the weevils' plight,
"So don't invite them to your night!"

All together, we sing a tune,
Under the watchful sun and moon.
With every bite, we feel so spry,
So let's have fun, oh me, oh my!

Cradled in Fruit's Embrace

Nestled 'neath an apple tree,
A private party, just for me!
With comfy leaves, a cozy nook,
I'm ready now, my favorite book.

But wait, what's that? A berry fight!
With giggling grapes and citrus bright.
They tumble down, make quite a mess,
I just can't leave, I must confess!

The fruits all sway with laughs and cheer,
In juicy dreams, we disappear.
Sweet nectar flows, a sticky race,
Where every smile is a warm embrace.

So when you're tired and feeling low,
Just find a fruit friend to let go.
With each delicious, zany bite,
You'll find that life is pure delight!

Juices of Time

Catch the drips of fruity lore,
As time spins on, we laugh and pour.
With every squeeze, a tale unfolds,
Of giggling fruit and secrets bold.

The lemon rolls with zesty flair,
While grapes concoct a jig with care.
Juice flows freely, no cares in sight,
A party brewing into the night.

We mix and blend with reckless glee,
Crafting potions as wild as can be.
"So, what's your flavor?" we jovially shout,
As citrus dreams swirl all about!

So take a glass, join the rhyme,
Savor the sweetness, the juices of time.
For every sip is a memory made,
A fruity fiesta, let's not be delayed!

Remnants of Sweetness

In the land of snacks and bites,
A fruit is found, oh what a sight!
With a crunch that sounds just so divine,
Left behind, the heart's a line.

Juice stains smudge the eager hand,
A bite of joy, a tasty brand.
To chew or toss, the question bends,
But who could waste what sweetness lends?

In a lunch box lies the tale,
Of savory mounds that might prevail.
Yet hidden still, the bits remain,
A cheeky grin when things fall plain.

Do ghosts of flavor haunt the peel?
As laughter rips like tasty meal.
So bite and giggle, love the core,
For what's inside, we can explore!

Circles of Life

Round and round the munching goes,
These little bites bring lots of woes.
A ring of joy, the laughter flows,
What's left behind? Well, no one knows!

The grass beneath, it holds the story,
Of pie and cider, all in glory.
But what of those who dare to thrive,
In circles made, they come alive.

The seeds may sprout a tree anew,
As joy spills forth in sunlit view.
Yet giggles linger, fruit in hand,
And lunchtime dreams spread 'cross the land.

So take a bite, don't be too shy,
Nonsense knocking, here's a pie!
With every munch and crunch to share,
Life's merry dance, we all declare!

Echoes in the Pulp

In the belly of the fruit, we find,
Stories echo, playful and unkind.
Juicy whispers, a giggle's trace,
What happens here, we can't replace.

Does laughter bounce within the skin?
With every bite, let the fun begin.
Mysteries hide in every nook,
A personality, the fruit's own book.

Oh, watch it drop from hungry hands,
It rolls and tumbles, oh how it stands!
In every pulp, a tale to tell,
Each chomp a laugh, a joyous swell.

The merry crunch, the seeds escape,
A fruit punchline in a silly shape.
So relish flavors, echoes loud,
In fruity fun, our hearts are proud!

Secrets in the Stem

Twirled around in nature's game,
The stem stands proud, it's not to blame.
For holding on to tales it knows,
As secrets drip where sunshine glows.

Peeling back the vibrant skin,
What's tucked inside? It's fun to spin.
With every nibble, a giggle bursts,
In every slice, a laugh that thirsts.

Hey, what's that near the hidden stem?
A tiny world in which we stem!
Creatures crawl from fruity lore,
Lost in the laughs they can't ignore.

So hold your fruit and give a cheer,
For every bite brings friends so near.
In the comical world of trees and vines,
There lies a treasure, oh how it shines!

Unraveled Threads of Nature

In the orchard where shadows play,
Squirrels plot their cheeky way.
Whispers dance on the breeze,
Tales of fruit, oh what a tease!

Beneath the trees, secrets unfold,
Forgotten stories, daring and bold.
A bite or two, the mischief brews,
Not just the apples, but amusing snooze!

Cider dreams in the air do swirl,
With hiccups and giggles, nature twirls.
A game of chase through the branches wide,
Laughing as the critters collide!

As the sun dips low, colors ignite,
Every crunch sparks comedic delight.
So here's to the fun of what lies in store,
All from the heart of a harmless core!

Beneath the Glimmering Surface

In the garden, a glint of cheer,
Juicy stories we love to hear.
Frogs don capes, on apples they hop,
Watch them dance till they flop!

Beneath the skin, a giggle hides,
Crisp with laughter when nature decides.
Roll on the ground, the fruit takes flight,
Under the moon, they throw a night light!

Chewing on clouds, tasting the fun,
Tickled by breezes that play and run.
The fruit knows jokes, they shimmer and shine,
In every bite, there's a silly line!

So take a nibble, and let out a cackle,
Nature's own jesters, with each little crackle.
For beneath the surface, hilarity hides,
In the twists and turns of what nature bides!

Essence of the Hidden Harvest

Deep in the maze of greenery bright,
Lies mischief wrapped tight in twilight.
The fruits peek out with a grin so wide,
Ready for shenanigans to glide!

Pies burst forth with laughter and cream,
While seeds plot a delicious dream.
Each slice holds a whimsical chance,
A fruity frolic, an impromptu dance!

Nibbles of joy in a cheerful feast,
Tangled in uproar, laughter increased.
From summer's joy to winter's glow,
A hidden party where giggles flow!

So gather around, let the humor pour,
In the hidden harvest, life's never a bore.
With each fruity morsel, a secret held dear,
A treasure trove of giggles, oh dear!

The Musings of a Fallen Fruit

Once a proud piece on the tree so grand,
Now a legend, rolling through the land.
With a plop on the ground, the fun begins,
Sharing its tales of giggles and grins!

Under the leaves, a jester takes leap,
Inciting chortles, promises to keep.
Spinning around in a fruity mess,
Life's little carnival, oh what a jest!

Beneath the moon, the laughter does soar,
Even the worms join in with a snore.
Each bruise tells a story of playful delight,
From the orchard's edge to the starry night!

So here's to the fun of that which cascades,
Fallen fruit knows the best escapades.
With a wink and a twist, let the laughter ignite,
For life is delicious, oh what a sight!

Fruit of Whispered Truths

In the orchard where gossip flows,
Fruit speaks secrets that nobody knows.
The pear giggles at the drapes of vines,
While cherries swap tales over fruity wines.

Beneath the shade, the berries conspire,
Sharing jokes that could set world ablaze.
The plump ones chuckle, they burst with pride,
While citrus grins with zest at their side.

Hidden within the Orchard

Among the trees, a riddle grows,
Whispers between the fruits in rows.
The lemons snicker, the apples giggle,
While peachy lines make everyone wiggle.

A cantaloupe claims it knows the score,
While mangoes dance, demanding more.
The berries vote for a festive spree,
While nuts just laugh, 'We're quite nutty, you see!'

Tales from the Seed

In a patch where secrets sprout and twirl,
Little seeds tell of the great big whirl.
A tiny sprout claims a pirate's fame,
While daring roots spread the silliest names.

From cherries, stories of starlit nights,
To squashy gossips that take flight.
Each seed a whisper, each vine a jest,
Even pumpkins think they're puffed-up best.

The Heart of Frosted Harvest

When winter wraps the bounty tight,
Fruits tell jokes in the frosty night.
A frosted berry dons a silly hat,
While whispers fly, 'What's chitter-chatter, bat?'

The squash hums a tune, off-key but bold,
With figgy friends sharing tales of old.
And there in the crisp, nostalgia rings,
As laughter warms all the chilly things.

Veils of Flavor and Design

In a world where bites disguise,
Each crunch brings laughter, oh what a surprise!
Wrapped in colors, bright and bold,
Tales of sweetness quietly unfold.

Crisp on the outside, soft within,
Funny how we laugh at the mess we're in.
Juicy tales drip down our chin,
With every nibble, mischief begins.

Seeds like secrets, hidden away,
Sprouting giggles with every play.
A peck here, a chomp there,
Disguised wisdom in flavors rare.

In this orchard of silly delights,
Each taste reveals new comic heights.
So take a bite and giggle some more,
For laughter's the prize in this fruity store.

Secrets Linger in the Orchard

Underneath the leafy green,
Lies a world quite unforeseen.
Crisp surprises with each chew,
Giggles hidden in the dew.

A cheeky grin, a stolen take,
Silly puns and careful fake.
Whispers swirl from tree to tree,
The humor spreads like sticky bee.

Tart or sweet, oh what a mix,
Unruly jokes that twist and fix.
Every bite a chuckling friend,
In the orchard, laughter won't end.

So gather round, take a chance,
Join the vegetative dance.
With every crunch, joy takes flight,
In this fruit-filled, funny night.

The Depths of a Juicy Mystery

In the center, secrets swirl,
A juicy plot begins to unfurl.
With each slice, stories emerge,
Tangled tales in a fruity surge.

Crimson hues and golden skin,
Hold mysteries tucked deep within.
Silly faces as juices burst,
The laughter grows, an unplanned thirst.

Nibbles taken, giggles grow,
What's inside? We'd love to know!
A punchline hidden, a core so bright,
This fruit's no regular delight.

So gather 'round, let's all partake,
In this juicy storyline we'll make.
As we dive deep, let laughter reign,
In this funny fruit parade, we'll gain!

Of Flesh and Forgotten Dreams

Once a dream in a tree so high,
Now a jester with a mischievous eye.
Taking bites of what was lost,
Every chuckle comes at a cost.

Flesh so tender, fit for a jest,
Funny moments put to the test.
From seeds of laughter, stories grow,
A comedy show in every row.

Forgotten dreams in every core,
With each laugh, we settle the score.
Juicy memories at the base,
In the orchard, humor finds its place.

So let us feast on joy tonight,
In every twinkle, there's delight.
With every crunch, the laughter beams,
As we unveil the fruit of dreams.

Unlocking Nature's Vault

In the orchard where laughter grows,
Tales of crunch and sauce expose.
The whispers of fruit, they start to play,
While squirrels plot their heist today.

Each bite reveals a playful jest,
Seeds of humor in nature's chest.
Giggling leaves, a secret spree,
Peeling laughter with glee and glee.

The juice drips down with a wink so sly,
A riddle's wrap in a fruity lie.
Biting in, we notice quirks,
Nature's comedy, it surely works!

So gather round for the fun parade,
In every morsel, a laugh is made.
With sticky fingers, we share the score,
In the orchard's heart, with secrets galore.

The Silent Fertility

In the garden where mischief lurks,
Fruits giggle in their leafy quirks.
With every round of nature's game,
Fruits feel no blush, they have no shame.

Underneath the blooms that sway,
Surprises linger, hiding in play.
As fruits conspire in sunny cheer,
The rustling branches lend an ear.

A fruit's round belly, with secrets packed,
Laughs in its skin, what fun it's cracked!
Nature chuckles with apple charm,
Each bite a giggle, so fresh and warm.

So dive in deep without despair,
In this orchard, it's all fair.
With bites of joy, we'll risk it all,
As the jests of nature rise and fall.

Hidden in Juicy Depths

Beneath the skin, a joke awaits,
A bite so crisp, it celebrates.
Inside the walls of fibrous grin,
Lies a burst of laughter, thick and thin.

Each slice revealed, a mystery,
With squirts of juice, it's history.
Drenched in sweetness, the puns unfold,
As silly tales of summer told.

With every wave of fruity cheer,
Nature's laughter rings sincere.
Tiny seeds sing a playful song,
Whispering secrets that can't go wrong.

Peel the layers, take a peek,
Each juicy giggle, a playful streak.
In strange terrain of ripe delight,
The humor blooms from day to night.

The Gravity of Spheres

Round and merry, the fruits roll near,
Chasing giggles, spreading cheer.
A playful bounce on the grassy floor,
As nature's mischief sings folklore.

Like planets dance in a jester's way,
These juicy orbs in their ballet.
They tumble forth in silly arcs,
Igniting laughter, bright sparks.

The world spins round with every twist,
In fruity realms, we can't resist.
With bites of fun, they take their flight,
In every crunch, pure delight.

So let us laugh at this fruit parade,
In nature's hands, the jokes are made.
Sphere by sphere, we roll along,
In the orchard's heart, a crazy song.

Whispering Seeds

In the garden's chatter, seeds conspire,
Jokes beneath the soil, they never tire.
A beetle's punchline, a worm's little dance,
Nature's jesters throw a silly romance.

Sprouting laughter, roots intertwine,
Tickled by the sun, oh how they shine!
Buds giggle quietly, petals in a row,
Sharing secrets only they would know.

Echoes of the Orchard

In the orchard's heart, giggles abound,
Fruits swap tales, stories resound.
A pear tries to tell, but an apple interrupts,
With a laugh that makes all the rest erupt.

Branches sway gently, like dancers in rhyme,
Their leafy laughter, a jolly chime.
"Did you hear that joke?" asks one little sprout,
"It's juicier than me, without a doubt!"

Beneath the Surface

Down below the ground, it's a riot,
Roots forming circles, having a diet.
"Did you hear about the pear that could sing?
It didn't have a clue, it just wore a bling!"

Worms feeling fancy, dressed in their best,
Throwing a party, they never rest.
Cheeky little radishes join the fun,
Swaying their tops in the evening sun.

Nature's Quiet Stories

In the rustling leaves, whispers abound,
Squirrels plotting as they scurry around.
"Where's the best spot for my winter loot?
I heard the grapes know a sweet little route!"

The daisies nod, oh what a sight,
As bees share tales of nectar delight.
Nature's quiet stories, all in a buzz,
Funny little secrets, just because!

Whispers in the Overripe Air

In the orchard where fruits might spill,
Laughter bounces from tree to hill.
Juicy gossip floats on the breeze,
As squirrels debate the best summer cheese.

Branches sag low, their whispers abound,
"Did you hear what the pear thought was profound?"
The plump peaches chuckle, and the berries grin,
While the jaded pines just roll their limbs in.

Bees buzz around, sharing frivolous tales,
Of juicy mishaps and fruity fails.
"Did that apple just fall, or has it lost its way?"
They cackle till sunset ends the day.

So join the fruit fiesta, take a bite or two,
There's humor in sweetness, laughter in dew.
In the overripe air where jokes spring to life,
Even the pumpkins giggle, ignoring some strife.

The Silent Language of Orchard Boughs.

Wobbly apples sway in a dance,
"Are you ripe enough to take a chance?"
The branches whisper soft and low,
"Oh, pick me first—I'm the star of the show!"

Leaves ruffle secrets, trading notes,
While ants march on in their tiny coats.
"Did you see that pear try to roll?"
"Quite the show-off, he thinks he's whole!"

The sun shines bright, casting playful glints,
As cherries gossip about the plump mints.
"Why's the banana hanging out with us?"
"Out of place, but who makes a fuss?"

In this fruit-filled world, life's a spree,
Where mischief is planted on every tree.
The silent boughs, they know the score,
In the orchard's laughter, we dare to explore.

Beneath the Crimson Skin

Beneath the skin of red and green,
Lies a world of giggles, unseen,
Fruits swap tales of their wildest dreams,
And chuckle at night beneath moonbeams.

Though oranges boast with zest and flair,
They can't match the wit of a juicy pear.
"I'm the sweetest," the nectarines claim,
But the blackberries shout, "We're full of fame!"

Hardy nuts listen, snickering low,
"Who's going to win this fruit-verse show?"
"Bite me, if you dare!" the bold cherries tease,
While bees hum choruses with perfect ease.

So peel back the laughter, let the fun in,
Find joy in each bite and the games we spin.
Beneath the crimson, life dances bright,
In a fruity carnival, day or night!

Whispers of the Orchard

In the orchard's heart where laughter starts,
Frisky fruits play their little parts.
"Pick me! Pick me!" the apples plead,
As rhymes weave through every seed.

Grapes gather 'round for a holiday cheer,
"Best not mention last year's reindeer!"
Lemons laugh, pucker up their faces,
While berries boast of their colorful graces.

The wind shakes branches with playful glee,
"Who knew fruit could be so free?"
Fruits shine bright in their dazzling hues,
All sharing tales of their silly views.

So take a stroll in the zesty air,
Laugh with the harvest, let go of care.
In the whispers of the orchard loud,
Find joy in each journey, feel so proud!

Roots of Enchantment

In a garden, things are spry,
Wiggly worms, oh my, oh my!
Twisting tales beneath the soil,
Laughing roots begin to toil.

Gnomes in hats, they dig and dance,
Crafting pranks with every chance.
Colors whirl from hidden trails,
Even carrots tell their tales!

Hidden in the Cradle

In shadows thick, the giggles hide,
Tiny tales of fruit collide.
Cradled dreams in leafy beds,
Whispers tickle tiny heads.

Potato sprites and onion gnomes,
Wandering far from garden homes.
They plot a feast, a joyous spread,
With fanciful thoughts, they dance instead!

The Life Before Bite

Before the crunch, the crisp delight,
Fruitful adventures took their flight.
Dancing dew drops, sunny days,
Routing through the wild maze.

Juicy jokes on branches swing,
Chasing clouds, we laugh and sing.
Life in trees was just the start,
Before the hand, it stole my heart!

Odes to Forgotten Flavors

In jars of jam, we find the past,
Fruits and laughs, a bond so vast.
Marmalade mishaps, squishy falls,
Flavor feuds in kitchen halls.

Fungi giggle, spices tease,
Jazzing up our pantry with ease.
Forgotten fruits in a dizzy swirl,
Bring a wink to every world!

The Taste of Forgotten Lore

Once a fruit with tales to tell,
In a basket, it went swell.
But now it's just a memory,
Tasting sweet, yet bitterly.

Worms tease secrets from its skin,
They giggle as they tuck right in.
A slice of laughter, a hint of woe,
In every bite, confusion grows!

Juicy whispers in every chew,
Of all the mischief it once knew.
The fruit that fell with all its pride,
Now slips on jokes and merry ride.

So take a bite and ponder this,
What treasures lie beneath the bliss?
For once it held a noble throne,
Now it's just a funny bone.

Beneath the Branches' Veil

Under branches, giggles bloom,
Where the ripe fruit met its doom.
Curious critters dance around,
In search for treasures to be found.

Leaves whisper jokes, so light and sly,
While squirrels plot as they sneak by.
Fuzzy thoughts in leafy shade,
A comedy show in nature played.

Watch the rascals, what a scene!
Nibbling snacks where they have been.
Each fallen piece, a grand charade,
Entertaining all who stayed.

So share a laugh and lift a cheer,
For nature's humor's always clear.
Beneath the veil, secrets swim,
In nature's tale, we all fit in.

The Seed's Silent Confession

Buried deep, a jest unfolds,
A seed with dreams, so bold yet cold.
It whispers softly to the ground,
"I'm more than just a meal, profound!"

In soil's embrace, it starts to grin,
With hopes of where it might have been.
But snails and bugs share gossip loud,
It's just a bus stop—oh so proud!

Through the dirt, it plans its rise,
To burst forth bright, to everyone's surprise.
Yet every sprout is met with glee,
"What's this surprise? A veggie spree?"

So ponder well, dear friends and kin,
A seed might just invite a spin.
Laugh out loud at the twisty fate,
For nature's seeds can feel so great!

Fragments of Enigmatic Bloom

In the garden of quirky tales,
Petals dance like silly sails.
Each bud a riddle, bright and sweet,
Promises made at the dew's greet.

One flower claims it knows a joke,
While others giggle, poke and poke.
Fragrance floating, fun in air,
A bloom might just drop wisdom bare.

If blossoms could talk at this hour,
They'd spill the beans on joyful power.
A sunbeam whispers, blooms reply,
Their secrets drifting 'neath the sky.

So gather round this flowered lore,
Where laughter blooms forevermore.
In nature's plot, dawn to dusk,
A fragrant joke, a fragrant husk.

Crumpled Petals

In a world where fruit is round,
Petals crumple, secrets found.
Laughing buds beneath the tree,
Whisper tales of joy and glee.

Worms in suits wear tiny hats,
Dancing with the garden cats.
Bees buzz loudly, jesters bold,
Telling stories never told.

Lemons tease with sour grin,
While cherries giggle, tuning in.
Life's a carnival, oh what fun,
Underneath the golden sun.

Petals crumple, dreams collide,
In this orchard, we abide.
Turn the page, let laughter soar,
Secrets tucked in petals' lore.

Consciousness of the Orchard

In the orchard, thoughts take flight,
Fruits debate by morning light.
Peaches whisper, 'life's a game!'
While nuts insist, 'We're not so lame!'

Trees in robes of leafy green,
Stir opinions, trends unseen.
Neighbors shout from branches high,
'What's the secret? Let us pry!'

Beneath the shade, a laughter burst,
As juicy gossip quenches thirst.
Ciders flow with every tale,
In this orchard, we prevail.

Orchard's thoughts are sweet and bright,
Mixing day with joyful night.
Life's peculiar, that's the score,
In this place, we search for more.

The Sweet Disguise

Under wraps of crimson hue,
Fruits pretend to be brand new.
Lemons sport a sunny grin,
While radishes tuck in their skin.

Plums wear shades for extra flair,
Mangoes strut; they do not care.
All around, a sneaky show,
Secrets hidden in the glow.

A fruit parade, quite the surprise,
With clever masks and sweet disguise.
Melons sing, while grapes revolve,
In the fun, they all dissolve.

Nature's jesters, light and bright,
Share their wisdom in the night.
Beneath the skins, the truth will slide,
In this harvest, joy's our guide.

Kernel Kisses

In a shell, a secret lies,
Popcorn dreams and sweet replies.
Kernel kisses, laughter streams,
Popping joy in sunlit beams.

Corny jokes from cob to ear,
Chasing woes and spreading cheer.
Pints of butter, heaps of salt,
Making every laugh exalt.

At the fair, we twirl and spin,
Sweet treats bring that grin again.
Kernels bursting with delight,
Laughter echoes through the night.

So pop the fun and share the glee,
In the warmth of harmony.
Kernel kisses, worth the taste,
In this joy, there's no waste.

Secrets Beneath the Skin

There once was a fruit with a tale so sly,
Hidden beneath where the cheeky worms lie.
Tasting the sweetness is just half the fun,
The other half's secrets, baked into a pun.

With every bite, a giggle can burst,
For under the surface, the mischief's rehearsed.
Juicy confessions that tickle your tongue,
Wrapped in the laughter of legends unsung.

So peel back the skin, take a peek inside,
Find the quirks where the funny ones hide.
A core filled with laughter, it makes perfect sense,
In the land of the snack, where jokes are immense.

Feel free to nibble, your laughter is sweet,
As nature designed it, a mischievous treat.
For every great secret that's waiting for you,
Is a punchline that spins in a whirl of bright hue.

Where the Juice Runs Deep

Juice droplets scatter with every good bite,
A squirt of delight that brings giggles to light.
In this playful fruit, where the mischief flows,
A splash of bright laughter, that nobody knows.

Dive in for the flavor, the shenanigans thrill,
Each taste, a sweet riddle, a playful chill.
Where juices keep running, like pranks in the air,
You might taste a chuckle, with a zing of despair.

Sharing a crunch makes the giggles arise,
Shadows of secrets with each juicy surprise.
Watered by laughter, the orchard runs wild,
Unlocking the humor of nature's own child.

So gather together beneath leafy roofs,
In the laughter of fruit, you'll find tasty truths.
For where the juice flows, it's fun guaranteed,
There's nothing so funny as nature's own deed.

Echoes of the Orchard

In the orchard we wander, where whispers do play,
Secrets are scattered in a fruity ballet.
Listen close, can you hear the giggle-filled breeze?
It dances with apples and tickles the trees.

Each tree holds its stories, both silly and wise,
With fruits wearing chuckles, disguising their size.
A whispering promise of laughter in stock,
The fruits bear the tales, like a punchline clock.

So take to the garden, surround yourself free,
Where echoes of laughter are just like a spree.
In every bright bite, a chuckle's bestowed,
In the laughter of greens, where secrets erode.

With every sweet crunch, let your joy take flight,
The orchard's alive with the quirkiest sights.
For where laughter echoes, the heart surely sings,
Join in the fun that each fruit brings.

Shattered Seeds of Knowledge

Seeds of bright wisdom scattered so neat,
Crack one open, an odd little treat.
They whisper the tales that make spirits soar,
In the cracks of their shells, there's humor galore.

Silly ideas sprout in the soil,
A giggle erupts where ideas uncoil.
With every good seed, there's a question at play,
Why did the fruit cross the bright, sunny way?

Pulling the truths from the roots that run deep,
Chasing the laughter, it's never too steep.
For knowledge is funny when shared with a grin,
Each slice of enlightenment, treasuring kin.

So scatter your seeds, let the laughter ignite,
In the garden of humor, everything's bright.
With every small chuckle, a lesson unfolds,
Shattered seeds of wisdom are treasures of gold.

The Unsung Ritual of the Bite

With a crunch, a laugh erupts,
A dance ignites, oh so abrupt.
A juicy plunder, sweet delight,
In this odd ritual, we take flight.

In gardens wide, where fruits parade,
We toast to bites, in full charade.
Each chomp a story, each chew a grin,
In this fruity game, we all win.

Circles formed in post-bite cheer,
Whispers of flavor, oh so clear.
We laugh at seeds that tripped our games,
In juicy laughter, we find our claims.

So grab a slice, don't hold it tight,
Share the joy, let's take a bite.
In every crunch, a secret hides,
In fruity merriment, laughter abides.

Pulped Memories of Fall

Barefoot in orchards, what a sight,
My friends and I, a silly flight.
We munch on treats, our cheeks aglow,
With each sweet bite, more memories flow.

Twirling leaves, the trees all sway,
We giggle loud, let worries stray.
With smudged faces, we declare,
Adventures found in juicy air.

In bushels piled, we see the gold,
Of laughter shared, and tales retold.
Each pulp-stained moment, oh what bliss,
Who knew fall's harvest could end like this?

So raise a fruit, let's toast the day,
With silly antics, we'll laugh away.
For in these days, we find the core,
Of friendship sweet, forevermore.

Layers of Sweet Deception

Beneath the skin, oh what a tale,
Secrets hid, they seldom fail.
Each bite reveals a plot so sly,
With every munch, we slyly pry.

A shiny red, but what's inside?
A juicy mess where truths collide.
We laugh at seeds, disguise misplaced,
In every twist, we're fondly laced.

In fruited dance, deception reigns,
With playful bites, we break the chains.
A wink exchanged as crumbs cascade,
Within the laughter, memories made.

So peel it back, the layers bare,
Discover wonders in the air.
In each cheeky grin, the secrets seep,
In fruity jest, we take the leap.

Shadows in the Crimson Flesh

In twilight hush, we gather round,
With bites and quips, and laughter's sound.
The shadows dance on crimson bright,
As secrets spill in jovial bite.

With fruit in hand, we tell our quests,
Of daring feats, our fruity tests.
Each chuckle echoes, robust and wide,
In juicy tales, our hearts abide.

The crimson glow, a playful quest,
As flavors swirl, we're truly blessed.
With every munch, new stories born,
In layered laughter, our souls adorn.

So join the feast, let shadows merge,
In fruity joy, we all emerge.
With every bite, we find our way,
In this delightful, silly play.

Wonders in the Pulp

In the land of bites and munch,
Where fruits are ripe, they love to crunch.
A mystery lurks in every slice,
With giggles held, oh, isn't it nice?

You bite and chew, then find the pit,
While squirrels giggle, a perfect fit.
Peels slip away like slippery fish,
The inner joke: a sweetened wish!

Juicy drips down a chin so bare,
A sticky mess, but no one cares.
Laughter echoes through the trees,
As we savor bites with giddy glee!

So here we munch, and laugh so loud,
In the orchard, we're all so proud.
Surprises wait beneath the skin,
With every crunch, let the fun begin!

The Veil of Sweetness

Behind the skin, a tale unfolds,
Of sugary secrets, brave and bold.
With sticky fingers, we dive right in,
Finding joy beneath the grin.

Juice flows freely in playful streams,
As dreams dance lightly in fruity beams.
The sweetness whispers through the air,
Drawing giggles, a tangled affair.

With every bite, we twist and twirl,
A wacky ride, a fruity whirl.
Masked in peels, the fun's concealed,
In each mauled piece, a truth revealed!

So come and join the fruity feast,
Where laughter sprouts, a juicy beast.
Nibbles shared bring us delight,
With sweetness dancing in the light!

Lost in the Orchard

In an orchard filled with sunlit glee,
We wander clueless, just you and me.
Chasing shadows, where tasty treats,
Hide their wonders in crunchy feats.

Underneath the branches, we sneak and peek,
Finding fruits with a glossy streak.
Laughter spills like juice on the ground,
When surprises pop up all around!

With every munch, a giggle springs,
As we twirl, forgetting our things.
In the chaos, we leap and glide,
In this fruity maze, we shall abide!

So let the fun continue here,
As we dance through laughter and cheer.
In the orchard's heart, we're forever caught,
In juicy joys, a sizzling thought!

The Unseen Core

Beneath the skin, the jesters hide,
A secret swirl we can't abide.
Each crisp bite leads to silly sights,
Dancing flavors ignite our nights.

Unraveling tales with every crunch,
Messy giggles, a perfect lunch.
The heart of fruit shall never show,
What makes the fun in bites that glow!

In colors bright, they play their ruse,
Tickling taste buds with fruity hues.
Cutting deeper, what do we find?
Laughter and sweetness, perfectly aligned!

So take a nibble, let the fun soar,
Discover joys we've yet to explore.
With every bite, our spirits soar,
Unseen secrets, we giggle for!

Revelations at Dusk

On a picnic blanket, we sat in delight,
Whispers of fruit spilled into the night.
A worm wore a hat, he danced in the sun,
Sipping on juice, he said, "Life's just begun!"

Under the apple trees, tales took their flight,
Of secretive munchers who nibble just right.
A giggle erupted when one said, "I swear,"
The fruit's tale is juicy, and no one should care!

As shadows grew longer, our chuckles did swell,
Each bite from the fruit held a story to tell.
And the seeds, oh the seeds, were gossiping too,
Sharing wild stories of sticky old goo!

So let's raise a toast to our fruity delight,
For those who dare nibble till they take flight.
With giggles and grins, we'll feast till we snore,
In the orchard, we'll dance 'round the half-eaten core!

The Sweetness Beneath

Beneath the thick skin hides laughter and cheer,
A crunchy delight we hold so dear.
With each juicy bite that we boldly explore,
The sweetness spills out, can't help but adore!

Ticklish and wiggly, the juice starts to flow,
While critters in tunnels put on a great show.
They giggle and chuckle, so sly and carefree,
"What's better than snacking? Come join us for tea!"

The shade of the branches feels just like a dream,
Where silliness drips like some caramel cream.
With shadows that dance and stories galore,
We feast like the critters, 'til we crave even more!

So munch on with glee, let the juice run down,
Wear sticky smiles like crowns, don't wear a frown.
For hidden delights in the orchard we seek,
Are shared in the laughter that makes our hearts peak!

Slices of Forgotten Lore

Once upon a time, or maybe it's now,
The legends of fruit made us laugh, take a bow.
Each slice tells a tale, so wacky and wild,
Of apples that giggle, oh, aren't they beguiled?

One slice revealed a secret so silly,
That fruits all wear socks—who knew? What a philly!
With whispers and chuckles, they snickered all night,
As the feasting continued, hearts filled with delight.

Old Granny Smith shared her tales so absurd,
Of apples on bikes, how they'd fly like a bird.
They flew 'round the clouds, having too much fun,
With the laughter of fruit echoing under the sun!

So here's to the slices with stories untold,
In every sweet morsel, let joy unfold.
For laughter's the seasoning, embrace all the lore,
As we munch on the tales of the fruit we adore!

Enchanted Layers

In the orchard of madness, we peel back the fun,
Each layer reveals a new joke on the run.
Beneath the bright skin hides a world full of glee,
With a giggle from fruits, oh come laugh with me!

The underbelly whispered of pranks to be planned,
With puns so ripe, they take us by hand.
A rogue little seed jumped up with a cheer,
Saying, "Knock, knock! Who's there? Froot, never fear!"

With laughter aplenty, we roll on the grass,
While the wise old tree swayed, letting time pass.
It winked with a twinkle as it showed us the chart,
Mapping the journey of joy in each part.

So let's delve through layers, unravel the jest,
For each crunchy layer will put you to test.
With laughter and fruit, what a magical score,
In this orchard of giggles, we'll always want more!

The Bitter and the Sweet

In orchards bright with sunny cheer,
A creature nibbles, oh so dear.
With every crunch, the laughter flows,
Yet seeds remind of squatty foes.

A giant worm with eyes so wide,
Claims half the fruit, oh what a ride!
He twirls and dances, thinks he's grand,
While juice drips down the sleazy land.

But one day he took a daring leap,
Into a fae's enchanted keep.
With giggles, she turned him into pie,
Now he just watches with a sigh.

So next time you munch on a treat,
Remember bites can be bittersweet.
Even the worm has dreams that soar,
In the land of the rotten, there's always more.

Disguised in Rustic Red

A jester sways in colors bright,
Dressed in skin of ruby delight.
With seeds to share, he makes a crack,
While squirrels scheme with sneaky knack.

"I'm just a fruit!" he shouts with glee,
"To hide my layers is the key."
But every smile hides a deep core,
Where secrets of sweetness wait to explore.

One day a lad took the bait,
A chomping sound sealed his fate.
The punchline hit! He felt the whack,
A rush of tart, with laughter back!

So when you see that shiny glaze,
Remember jesters have their ways.
In bites of joy, with every shred,
The tales of humor are widely spread.

The Cradle of Forbidden Secrets

In the shade of leafy chatter,
A whisper weaves, it climbs and flatter.
Beneath the skin of crimson hue,
Lies a mystery too weird to chew.

With giggles caught in cheeky flare,
A tale unfolds, oh who would dare?
For inside one fruit, not sweet but sly,
Lurks a riddle that makes you cry.

The wise old owl perches near,
He hoots a pun for all to hear.
"Deceit is not just in the stew,
Even pure seeds can twist and skew!"

So heed the fruit that wears a grin,
It might just hint at the chaos within.
With every bite a tale is cracked,
Of faux-pas wrapped and antics packed.

Adventures in Cycles of Decay

In the garden, a tale unfolds,
As wrinkled skins are left in molds.
With laughter echoing in the breeze,
The dance of rot, it aims to please.

The bumpy fruits in varied states,
Hold stories of their wobbly fates.
With ants in hats and grins all around,
They boast of battles, both lost and found.

An old tree leans, it starts to sing,
Of all the joys that decay can bring.
With peeling laughs and raucous sights,
Life's a cycle, filled with delights.

So toss that skin into the breeze,
Join the fun in the rot of trees.
For every end, a new laugh grows,
In the chaos where nature throws.

www.ingramcontent.com/pod-product-compliance
Lightning Source LLC
Chambersburg PA
CBHW060131230426
43661CB00003B/386